10 WAYS TO CREATE LESS WASTE

by Mary Boone

PEBBLE
a capstone imprint

Published by Pebble, an imprint of Capstone
1710 Roe Crest Drive, North Mankato, Minnesota 56003
capstonepub.com

Copyright © 2024 by Capstone. All rights reserved. No part of this publication may be reproduced in whole or in part, or stored in a retrieval system, or transmitted in any form or by any means, electronic, mechanical, photocopying, recording, or otherwise, without written permission of the publisher.

Library of Congress Cataloging-in-Publication Data is available on the Library of Congress website.

ISBN: 9780756577971 (hardcover)
ISBN: 9780756578206 (paperback)
ISBN: 9780756578015 (ebook PDF)

Summary: Did you know the average American creates more than 4 pounds of waste per day? Check out these 10 easy ways to cut your trash output, plus an activity to help you do so. Find out what tips work for you and spread the word. Together, we can make a difference!

Editorial Credits
Editor: Mandy R. Robbins; Designer: Heidi Thompson; Media Researcher: Jo Miller; Production Specialist: Tori Abraham

Image Credits
Getty Images: Carol Yepes, 17, FatCamera, 15, Jamie Grill, 18, kali9, Cover (bottom right), Lucy Lambriex, 16, Maksim Safaniuk, 9, natalie_board, Cover (bottom left), Wavebreakmedia, 12; Shutterstock: aslysun, 10, aslysun, Cover (top right), Elizaveta Galitckaia, 19, Esich Elena, 14, Kolpakova Daria, 13, Marijus Auruskevicius, 21, Nokuro, 7, PapatoniC, Cover (top left), SewCreamStudio, 11

All internet sites appearing in back matter were available and accurate when this book was sent to press.

Printed and bound in China. 5593

TABLE OF CONTENTS

What Is Waste? 4

How Much Waste Is There? 6

Waste Problems 8

10 Ways You Can Create Less Waste 10

Activity: Track Your Trash 20

    Glossary 22

    Read More 23

    Internet Sites 23

    Index 24

    About the Author 24

Words in **BOLD** are in the glossary.

WHAT IS WASTE?

Waste is anything we throw away. Spoiled food is waste. A broken toy is waste. So is an empty juice box. Waste is stuff we want to get rid of.

HOW MUCH WASTE IS THERE?

The average person in the United States makes 1,642 pounds (745 kilograms) of waste per year! That's a lot. It's the same weight as nine adult kangaroos! Where does all that waste go?

WASTE PROBLEMS

Garbage trucks take waste to the **landfill**. Waste gives off harmful **chemicals** as it breaks down. The chemicals go into the soil. They pollute the air. They get into the water. Making less waste is a way to help.

10 WAYS YOU CAN CREATE LESS WASTE

1. Get a **recycle** bin. Learn what packaging can be recycled where you live. Separate these items from waste. Plastic water bottles can be recycled. So can boxes, jars, and cans. Soon, recycling will be a habit!

2. Packaging isn't the only thing you can recycle. Don't throw away toys or clothes you've outgrown. Give them to friends. Or **donate** them to a **charity** or a second-hand store.

3. Water is another thing people waste. Take shorter showers. Turn off the water when you brush your teeth.

4. Ask your family to **compost**. Food scraps can go into a compost pile in your yard. Or you can use an indoor compost bin. Natural materials like vegetable peels will break down. They can help plants grow better.

5. Pack a **zero-waste** lunch. Carry a lunch box instead of a paper bag. Choose reusable containers instead of plastic bags. Skip the juice box. Use a refillable water bottle.

6. When you need clothes, shop at a second-hand store. Many clothes there are almost like new. Plus, it keeps those clothes out of the landfill. Resale shops can be great places to find toys or sports equipment.

7. Feeling creative? Make art projects using recycled materials. Paint on a piece of cardboard. Use fabric scraps to decorate a card.

8. Reuse paper. We often use one side of a piece of paper. Keep it and use the other side. Use it for math practice. Use it to write a list. You'll waste less. And you'll help save trees.

9. Don't waste electricity. Turn off the lights when you leave a room. Turn off the TV and computer when you aren't using them.

10. Talk to your friends and family about creating less waste. Tell them how small changes can make a big difference. Working together, you can help save the planet!

ACTIVITY: TRACK YOUR TRASH

Make a chart to track what you're throwing away. You can do this with your family or your class at school. Do it for a week.

How many of these items could be recycled? Could some be composted? Make changes. Track your trash again in a month to see if you've made improvements.

Item	Can this be recycled?	Can this be composted?	Can I replace this with an earth-friendly product?
Plastic straw	No	No	I could skip the straw.
Apple core	No	Yes	

21

GLOSSARY

charity (CHAYR-uh-tee)—a group that raises money or collects goods to help people in need

chemical (KE-muh-kuhl)—relating to the basic substances that make up all materials

compost (KOM-pohst)—to mix rotting leaves, vegetables, manure, and other items to be added to soil to make it richer

donate (DOH-nate)—to give something as a gift to a charity or cause

landfill (LAND-fil)—a system of trash and garbage disposal in which the waste is buried between layers of earth

recycle (ree-SYE-kuhl)—to make used items into new products; people can recycle items such as rubber, glass, plastic, and aluminum

zero-waste (ZEE-roe-WAYSTE)—creating little to no waste

READ MORE

French, Jess. *What a Waste: Trash, Recycling, and Protecting our Planet.* London: DK Children, 2019.

MacLachlan, Patricia. *My Friend Earth.* San Francisco: Chronicle Books, 2020.

Taylor, Anna. *Old Enough to Save the Planet.* London: Magic Cat, 2020.

INTERNET SITES

Kids' Stuff About Waste Reduction and Recycling
calrecycle.ca.gov/kids/

Recycle City
epa.gov/recyclecity/

Zero Waste Kids
towardzerowaste.org/learn/zero-waste-kids/

INDEX

art projects, 16

composting, 13, 20, 21

electricity, 18

garbage trucks, 8

landfills, 8, 15

packaging, 10, 11
paper, 14, 17
pollution, 8

recycle bins, 10
recycling, 10, 11, 16, 20, 21
resale shops, 15
reusable containers, 14

second-hand stores, 11, 15

water, 8, 10, 12, 14

zero-waste, 14

ABOUT THE AUTHOR

Mary Boone has written more than 65 nonfiction books for young readers, ranging from biographies to how-to craft guides. She grew up in rural Iowa. She now lives in Tacoma, Washington, with her husband, Mitch, and children, Eve and Eli. Mary loves being outdoors, reading, and hanging out with her Airedale terrier, Ruthie Bader.